Long Exposure

Cole Zimmerman

BookLeaf Publishing

India | USA | UK

Presentation by *BookLeaf Publishing*

Web: www.bookleafpub.com

E-mail: info@bookleafpub.com

ISBN: 9789358318784

First edition 2023

For everyone who has ever read one of my poems

The Way the Wilderness Torments Me with Visions of You

The wind whistles in my ears & I am my own
cavern.
it reminds me of your incessant lazy singing
while cooking, hunched over the woodburn
stove

The mountains have always been indifferent, but
today they are cruel
they jostle me around & dart out of reach, parrot
your laugh back to me,
form stony hands with your calluses,
stroke my cheek.

The shadows on the rocks perform an
interpretive dance
they replay all our dark moments,   rise like your
voice in anger   &   fade just like you,
somber

The clouds don't stoop down to illusions
I wish they would.

I wish they morphed themselves into
approximations of your different facial
expressions
just so I could see your inquiring eyes again
or the uptick in your lips that formed when you
were holding in a laugh
I'd beg them to lean down so I could finally run
a quarter through the furrows of your furious
eyebrows
But they do nothing, they stare at me expectantly
As if that will stop me from longing for you.

My way of missing you burns like a bonfire, I
want to get closer,
I want to warm my shivering hands…
I am pushed away. I went too close. Dangerous.

The dirt mixes in with my sweat until I am
caked in mud
I collapse on the ground & sob
The trees reluctantly stick out their branches to
trace comforting circles on my back

What do they want from me? For amnesia to
settle over me like a weighted blanket?
As if anything could make me forget you.

The flood overtakes me

I am a fly at the mercy of a rushing thrushing
river
I am lost to the throws of reminiscing

The waterfall looms ahead, I look forward to
weightlessness
I have finally been funneled out, squeezed each
drop until there's nothing but you.   You,
you, you,
you relentless current, intolerant & irate, willful
& wonderful, you make drowning feel like
flying.

( )

I will wash up by the thistles & briars
I hope you come to find me.

Attempting To Translate German Words With No Translation

Handschuhschneeballwerfer: a person who
throws snowballs with gloves on
When the snow never stops
I have lost my gloves, I am hardened
I am snow packed and frozen over
I am grabbing handfuls and cherishing the sting
I am starting to feel pain like awareness

Verschlimmbessern: to make something worse
by trying to improve it
Days are fine until they are unbearable
I gather wounds
like flowers, like collectibles
my apocalypse lands littered with carcasses,
with jutting rocks, with my unending process of
burning and breathing a broken propagation

Gemütlich: Heart, mind, temper, feeling
The sun bursts through gaps of clouds and kisses
my weary face
I am trying not to put this all on you and
I am failing, I am seeking out warmth moth-like,

I am running into fluorescent lighting, I am
clasping on for
a minute too long, the fire crackles and the wood
shifts and roars, I am coming back
I am, I am, I am,

Around 10 PM on Tuesday, May 13th, 2003

She has so many things she has to learn
but that's not what I'm thinking about right now.
I'm thinking about how her fingers look like
oversized worms
       how her head is shaped like an
apricot,
       how her nose is like a pig snout,
       how her face crumples in an ugly cry
       how she kicks and rears her legs as if
testing new nerve endings,
       how her feet are barely the size of my
palm
I'm thinking about how small she is, of course.
and
            how small she looks
in the doctor's arms carrying her away from me

My husband is by my side stroking my hair out
of my face
"No more." I tell him.
He laughs

He's probably thinking about how exhausted and
sweaty I look. Or maybe

he's also thinking about the way her eyes
focused on our faces,
as if she completely understood this whole
situation
Maybe he also half expected her to say
"Hello Mother and Father, it's lovely to meet
you."
She certainly said that with her eyes

Or maybe he's also replaying that moment,
that brief moment when she stopped crying
Swaddled in my arms, looking up at our faces
squished together
that brief moment when she smiled
her one tooth glinting in the hospital light
her tongue wiggling impatiently

As if she knew that soon her smile would
be like the first beam of morning light
and she wanted to get on with it already

Fellowship

I climb this mountain being told that he is here
to save me
I feel no hands; no kind smile;
sweat drips into my eyes
I go blind.
I will not wait for a phantom hand.
I can hike by myself
and that's what I will do.

Am No Artist

[the night gets painted in sickly shades of yellow
& am ceiling fan sprawled
Beat down by broom like dust from rug
The office of mind works into late hours

& wake on the page
the day's daze of browns and grays
Possess a flamingo grace

Focus
it's all

out of focus]

It's not that big of a deal.
Why are you upset?

Pale yellow mid-morning light juts through the
window
bathing hanging gutted animal carcasses in a
misaligned warmth.
gory gemstone
What say you to the luster sir?
nothing like it, nothing like it

Tall tall hats in gambling clubs
Men guffawing over the fact that nothing rips
out their insides
gleefully subservient to their own desires.
Clinks of ice in brandy glasses, straighten your
cravat,
glare at the nine of clubs like it insulted your
father

A man must keep his wits about him.
Painters paint, writers write, scholars scholar
with boyish heretofore
Truly extraordinary, the masculine grace
displayed…
A boorish third limb to swiften steps, to piss and
pinwheel,

to stick into deserts and twitch with no rhythm.

A black cat bats at the cow carcess's tail.
"Shoo, shoo you scoundrel!" the butcher chases
the curious creature away.
He sets up his work on sawing off the perfect
cuts, he begins to whistle.
"Papa!!!" his son comes running in, his mouth
stained from stolen sweets. He does a quick lap
around his father, a flurry of joyous motion. He
is being chased by young Isabella whose giggles
stop abruptly as she reaches the doorway.

Isabella was not warned about what she would
be running into.
She smells a vibrant dominating rot, she sees
bright red innards all twisted up in unfamiliar
misshapen shapes, she hears the subtle drip drip
of unstopping blood on the stone floor.

She screams.

Cleaning &
Cooking–Cooking &
Cleaning–

When God made Eve, he took a rib from
Adam's stomach;
I wonder if he knew then, how this action would
forever make men incompetent. How they would
take this rib and make
her a lesson in contradictions. We all know this;
she must do
everything while being nothing.

My brother is 32 and he doesn't know how to
cook, I opened up
his fridge and only found a Papa Murphy's pizza
box with a single old slice.
He sleeps on the couch most days, perhaps
because his bed feels empty.
My brother grasps onto his sense of empathy.
I boil water for pasta in his kitchen.

My father eats microwavable meals when Mom
works late.
When he does the laundry he mixes up all the
colors, and I sit and watch the red dyes

float up and out of his button-up, into
his undershirts, and they
come out splattered in pink splotches–
like unicorn blood– and when he takes
them out I wonder if he will forget what
he's done and blame Mom.

When you call, I no longer know what to say

In the chill of winter I was stretched out. I
am sorry, my strings are
fraying. I am not what I once was.

I think back on it– that
beautiful cacophony we shared as our strings
rang out, delving in to
colorful and deep like watching light play across
a film of soap. We
were in bubbles of perfect harmony, that
burst. I am sorry. My frets are
weathered now. I am not
what I once was.

I am dusty from disuse, I am scratched up and
you are still in pristine condition somehow. How
can you do that? How can your music be so
much
better when the only tangible difference is that
it is yours and not mine

I am sorry.
I don't think
I can stay

in tune.
I am not what
I once
was.

i am certain i said hi too loud and now you never want to look at me again

this is how i picture us
braided together
i am so close to your face and i steal your smile
and imprint it on my soul
(god your smile)

in my childhood home, there was this chest with
nothing in it: dark wood
and ornate, a burgundy interior. i would
continually open it up and check–
i think if i went back i would find you in there
(hidden and cherished)

this is how i see us
in the two ducks alone in the pond, circling each
other and almost giggling
in sunset clouds; in pockets of color
(i am altogether too enamored, you must see it)

i tend you like a secret
i dive into your meaning
i have forgotten what it means to be hopeful
(i am hopeful)

The Hold You Have On Me

After years, weeks, and nights of violent
thrashing–
my heart has finally broken through skin.
You once said I wore it on my chest.
You were right, of course
You were always right.

The Feast

You shriek with glee and look at me with your
saucer wide eyes smeared in empathy
you wield it like a weapon while,
you ponder what possibly happened to,
this despicable dithering thing dying on your
dissection table and
with the softness of a saber tooth tiger, you
scrape my stomach lining for scraps.
Taking and taking and taking and taking
Insatiable, you suck on my intestines like a straw
holding my heart in your hardened hands you
grin and start gulping and guzzling my blood
and it is not enough.
You butcher me with the grace of a wild boar
My fingers get deep fried; my thighs grilled; my
nose baked into pie;
And we dine at the fancy dining table.
You, with a kiss the cook apron on, at the head
and me, just a brain, at the end
the only part that was so rotten
that you simply couldn't
Eat it.

Complexities of Yellow

A sheen
A layer of smoke and smoke and smoke
The faint light of the lamp paints her like an old
painting
The candlelight flickers on her desk
She lowers her voice sometimes
just a little

massive

i am massive in the mountains!!
i am oh so so giant!
i stretch my arms out and reach peak to peak
some bears use my boots as a hibernation cave,
a bird tried to make a nest in my nostril the other
day

i learn the range,
trace the graves,
let them settle into the grooves of my fingertips.

sometimes i think about being small...
being oh so so small i had to look up
at my father to get him to bring his hand down to
mine.

i think if i leave i will shrink
wrap around myself and fold til impossible
like paper
torn up and succumbing to a wayward breeze.

but, for now, i am massive in the mountains.
and when i scream into the wind-
it screams back.

If not heaven, where do grandmas go

She was a constant wave on the Southern
coastline
I am saying was here prematurely,
to get used to the fact.
it was never a question before.

She was a stubborn orange leaf in upstate New
York,
She had been underappreciated,
and now I can't appreciate her.
like a puppy who destroyed an expensive toy
immediately,
Now looking up and wondering is that it?
Why have I done this?
I am picturing her in the hospital with oxygen
tubes;
I am trying to force the scent of her perfume
back into my nostrils;
I am looking at old pictures and begging them to
move.

She is almost dead in a North Carolina hospital
my love scatters to her like dust in the wind
it'll stick to her clothes;

it'll float by at her funeral;
it'll be in the dirt where she's buried.

On June 7th, she is a memory
and I am guilty
The rain never ceases
and I am guilty.

It's too complicated– I love her

we would turn hopscotch into block long
obstacle courses
jumping and twirling and chasing after each
other across the sidewalk

i think about it often–the amount of times i've
killed my mother

the saying morphed somehow, in the
neighborhood
to immediate death.

and our hopscotch obstacles morphed into
chance executions
as i hopped from guilty to grateful

arriving at the front door and wondering what i
have done

and she's smiling, and i'm 8 years old and 18,
and i'm trying to
reconcile with the fact that i love her, and i feel
her love and
it hurts– I feel her love and it hurts.

In the summer...

june and july blend together in a catastrophe of
watermelon juice and wildflowers
tree root arms that spider out
slicked with rain water
gasps of vacant time where the sun is the sky
minutes that dart out of reach from awaiting
hands
like fireflies

or perhaps it's something about starting with a
"j" and a "u"
and having 4 letters.

In the fall…

In the fall, ivy turns red only for a week or so
then it browns and shrivels.
Hangs slain on the vine

Sometimes I walk until nothing is familiar
I see the trees change; I see the cycle of seasons
over and
over. Sometimes these walks feel like
timelapses.

Trees do not change together, some are
full green–young. One is completely naked,
most are in some
stage of yellow and looking at their neighbors;
wondering if they are wrong.

I feel a kinship with forests, I also often
become so dense and wooden that I cannot see
the sun.
I have no clear paths, I continue until I am cut
down.

In the winter...

the sky always holds a bit of light when
the snow never ceases; i am looking out
on white rooftops; i am looking out into
lives lived and cruelly measuring mine

in the deep deep banks; the moon looks like
a lens flare; a focal point in the gray tinted
white of the sky; i am trudging through the
unmelted remains; and it is slow slow going

i am hoping for an avalanche; for a rapid
undertaking; for a chaotic moment of
reckoning; to be encased and incapacitated
i am hoping for a chance to hold myself

and when the cold consumes me;
i will feel a certain sense of peace;
i will know i have been everything that i could
be;
and that is beautiful.